The
Human Touch

By
Carleton Everett Knox

The Knox Art Co.
616 Broadway
Kansas City, Mo.

Index

Poems of Philosophy

Index

Poems of Sentiment

Index

Poems of Nature

Poems of Affirmation

The Human Touch

True happiness is found within,
Our souls are fed by such.
But while we tarry here on earth
We'll need the human touch.

Opportunity

If your yesterday proved a failure,
Just try it again today,
Opportunity stands close beside you, just now
It never is far away;
Then profit by yesterday's error,
Place mistakes down under your feet,
They will help you to rise
Toward the blue vaulted skies,
And you'll WIN in the face of defeat.

Weeds

A weed's a flower gone astray;
Methinks that in some bygone day
It bloomed in garden fair,
And I've a tho't if we'd but give
It love and tender care,
It's wondrous beauty and perfume,
The glory of it's perfect bloom,
Again would fill the air.

So 'tis with man we judge as bad;
I sometimes think had he but had
An outstretched hand to touch,
He might have found new grip on life
To succor him in time of strife;
And man of worth and power he'd be,
Had we but helped, just you and me,
By proffering human touch.

Charity

Charity means not alone
The adding gold unto one's purse
Who needs of food and shelter warm.
Unto my mind, he needs it worse
Whose name's assailed by friend or foe;
Who takes snap judgment on an act
Of which he does not know.

Prize Is Waiting Just Ahead for You

When the world is looking blue,
And your plans are all askew,
And you hardly know which way you best had
　　turn,
　Brace your shoulders, lift your chin,
　Smooth that frown and grin, boy, grin.
Prize is waiting just ahead for you.

Race is won in the last heat,
And the favorite oft is beat
When he slacks his pace in thinking he has won.
　Keep on humpin' every day,
　In the end you'll find 'twill pay.
Prize is waiting just ahead for you.

Hope's the biggest word I know,
Every doubt 'twill quickly throw
In wrestling match, where rules are well ob-
　　served.
　In the fray you'll need your muscle,
　For 'twill be no easy tussle,
But the prize is waiting just ahead for you.

Worth While

Face the world with a smile—
Life's always worth while.
　　To the fearless is given a crown.
Keep out the past—
Disappointments can't last,
　　Success was ne'er won by a frown.

Success

Success is won if we do our part
With a steadfast eye and a fearless heart,
With never a thot of failure's share,
But with purpose bold to do and dare.

With eyes turned ever toward shining sun,
We'll finish each task e're another's begun;
With never a whimper, with never a fear,
But with voice attuned to manly cheer.

A smile is an ally of true success,
While a frown will a weary soul oppress;
A cheery word will your task beguile,
Success is achieved thru work and thru smile.

Today the Best of All

Let's make today the best of all,
Let's answer every inward call
That leads to better living.
Let's strive anew for what is best,
Let's succor give to those opprest,
Our gain is in the giving.

This Is Life

A little sun, a little rain,
A little joy, a little pain,
A song of praise, a dirge's strain,
    And this is life.

Sometimes a crown, sometimes a cross,
Sometimes pure gold and sometimes dross,
Sometimes it's gain and sometimes loss,
    And this is life.

Sometimes we're good and sometimes bad,
Sometimes we're happy, sometimes sad,
Sometimes good humored, sometimes mad,
    And this is life.

Some poverty and then some wealth,
Some days of pain and some of health.
Some days of frankness, some of stealth,
    And this is life.

A little wrong, a little right,
A little day, a little night,
A bit of shade, then all is light,
    And this is life.

Problems

The greatest problems we confront
Are away off in the distance,
But by the time we meet them square
They offer no resistance.

Brotherhood

I count that day well spent, when I
   Can hope inspire, or courage bring
To one, who's fighting 'gainst great odds,
   Who's found in life naught but the sting.

When I can feel an answering throb
   In hand clasp, or can catch a smile,
I know I've touched his heart of hearts—
   He's grasped the thot that life's worth while.

The inspiration I would give
   Comes back to me at such a time,
Brings strength of purpose to my life,
   While common things are made sublime.

In giving freely we receive
   The very things we fain would give!
While pointing others to the road,
   We, too, in turn are taught to live!

When One Loves

When one loves no service seems too hard,
For in doing unto others we receive of our
reward.
Love lightens every burden; turns darkness
into day;
Love leads us upwards, bids us hope;
Love guards our lives alway.

Face the Old World With a Grin

When the problems in life seem too many,
  And you scarcely know where to begin,
Just throw back your shoulders, and swallow
      that sob,
  And face this old world with a grin!

When weary of toil and of trouble,
  When tired of the pleasures of sin,
Turn your face t'ward the sun, and the battle's
      half won
  If you face this old world with a grin!

When friends of your childhood forsake you,
  When harmony's lost in life's din,
Just buck up my boy, for there's lots of keen joy,
  If you face this old world with a grin!

Truth

Today the world is seeking Truth;
Not mere belief will satisfy the hungry soul;
And Truth is found in proving
Whether thing be right or wrong.
Today we're not content in knowing but a part;
We seek the whole.

Best Thoughts

Let's have more faith in all mankind, as thru
    the world we go.
For faith breeds hope,
    And hope breeds love—
'Twould Heaven make here below.

Let's have a smile for tear-dimmed eyes,
    A hand clasp warm and true.
A kind word given now and then
    Would help life's journey thru:

Let's think pure thoughts; let's use clean words;
    Face wrong with fearless eyes!
Let's stand for right, and all that's good,
    Our face turned toward the skies!

The Man Who Wins

The man who grins
Is the man who wins,
'Tis a slogan that's good every day,
While the man with a grump
Gets the awfulest bump,
So grin—you'll find it will pay.

Grin

Did you ever stop and ponder
  What a cheery grin would do,
Not only to the other chap,
  But likewise unto you?
I'd liken it unto a glass
  Reflecting back to view,
The smile or frown you gave to it—
  It's strictly up to you.

A cheery "Howdy" helps a lot
  To stranger in far land,
It sort o' cheers him on his way
  As touch of outstretched hand;
For lonesomeness is not alone
  Found far from haunts of men,
But in the city's hurrying throng
  I've felt its presence then.

It doesn't cost a single cent
  To pucker up and grin,
And somehow I can't help but think
  It more or less a sin
To never give a cheery smile,
  Nor bid a "Howdy-do"
To one who's lonesome-like and sad;
  So grin—'twill help you, too.

A Hand Clasp

Here's my hand across the distance,
Wishes best I send;
Tho' skies be bright or skies be gray,
Just count me as your friend.

A Friendly Hand

Methinks 'twill little matter at the end of life's
      long day
How much of gold we've gathered here below.
No matter how we've striven and no matter what
      we've won,
Unless we've shown some kindness to the poor
      and weary one,
We'll find at close of life it didn't pay.

I think I'd rather find just then the touch of
      friendly hand,
Of one I'd succor given here below;
I'd rather look into his eyes and hear his word
      of cheer
Than hold the wealth of Midas mine, aye, all the
      wealth down here,
I'd give it all for touch of friendly hand.

The Greatest Things

The greatest things in this world of ours
Are the things you'd perhaps call small,
But a kind word here,
And a smile given there
Will banish the trouble and sorrow and care
Of many a weary soul.

Whistle an Old Time Tune

*When blue and discouraged, when business
    is bad
    When everything goes dead wrong,
It's yourself that's to blame—just get in the
    game,
    And whistle an old time song!*

*When clouds of despair seem to hover close by,
    If you would change midnight to noon.
Just screw up your face with the best of good
    grace,
    And whistle a cheery old tune!*

*There are friends who'll desert you, when old
    age creeps on,
    When your feet are beginning to slip,
But just you show sand, for the end will be
    grand,
    Should you die with a song on your lip!*

Hope

Keep Hope abloom and every wish
   Your hungering heart desires,
Will come and be a part of you
   When warmed by Hope's bright fires,
Eternal Youth, the love of Man,
   The knowledge of a well spent Life,
Will all be yours to have and to hold,
   And peace be yours instead of strife.

Dreams Do Come True

Dreams do come true. Long years ago
I dreamed that some day I might stand
Before great throngs of people in this land
And give to them a message of good cheer,
Might bring to them a new-born hope,
Might break the fetters strong of
            Doubt and Fear.

Dreams do come true. Tonight I stood
Before a thousand listening men, eager to hear
The message brot—A message of good cheer,
With hearts all eager and in tune with mine,
I found within the throng response to soul,
A stimulant it brot to me—of love—of love
            Divine.

Dreams do come true. The spark of love
I dreamed that might be mine, I found
            tonight
In giving it to others. And the light
I longed to kindle in the breasts of men
Shows bright and clear as Sun's strong rays
This message of good cheer, I now can better
            give by lips and pen.

Close of Day

Thank God for peace that comes at close of day,
When all our petty cares are laid away;
When quiet reigns, when earth is hushed in sleep,
God sendeth then His messengers, their watchful
*   care to keep.*
And then when morning dawns and day re-
*   turns again,*
He gives us strength to do our daily task,
And balm we find to heal our every pain.

A Morning Thought

A bright new world is ushered in
    Each morn at rise of sun;
Our yesterdays are past and gone,
    A new life has begun.
So see to it our best we do
    Just now, nor morrow wait,
For should we put it off till then,
    We'll be one day too late.

Don't worry then, of days gone by
    Nor those that are to be;
The only time of which we're sure,
    Is NOW; So let us see
Improvement every day and hour,
    And at the set of sun
We'll words of approbation hear,
    And they will be, "WELL DONE."

Our Very Best

If we but do our very best,
We need not worry. All the rest
That we deserve, will us be given,
For harmony, indeed, is Heaven!
We have no tasks too great to bear,
So we need never have a care,
For strength we will receive each day
To bear our burdens all the way.
Don't worry then, nor be downcast;
The Present's ours, but not the Past!
Today's a fresh beginning here,
So labor on, and never fear.

The Bit of an Old Time Tune

Did you ever get up in the early morn
After a sleepless night,
To find that everything went dead wrong,
Not a bloomin' thing went right?
I've found the same the many a time
But I'll give you a cure for it—
Jes' whistle the bit of an old time tune
And the first thing you know—you'll forget.

Did you ever think business had gone to smash
When you'd lost on a venture bad,
When you'd staked your all on the turn of a trick,
Lost the last red cent you had?
If so, the thing that will help the most
At least I've found it true
Is to whistle the bit of an old time tune
Buck up and begin anew.

Git Up and Git

Don't ever say quit,
A better word's—Git!
A git-up-and-gitter sounds better!
  Don't ever say fail,
  Nor your sad lot bewail;
Be a git-up-and-gitter—that's better!

Don't ever say die!
A better word's—Try!
Just try and you surely will win;
  Forget all your sighin',
  Cut out all your cryin'!
Just try and you surely will win!

Fellowship

If I can help my fellow man
  By thot or word or deed,
I'll feel my life has been well spent,
  I'll worry not of creed.

If I can bring a smile of joy
  To eyes bedimmed with tears,
I'll worry not of sects or isms,
  I'll free my thots from fears.

If I can lend a helping hand
  To one less strong than I,
Of heaven I'll reap here on this earth,
  Not in some distant sky.

The Heart of a Friend

Some people find pleasure in hoarding up gold,
  While others find joy in the spending of it;
But they'll find at the end of life's long, winding
    trail
  That the hoarding or spending didn't matter
    one bit.

The big thing in life is in helping mankind,
  The joy that stays with us, that lasts till the end
Will be ours. And a peace outweighing all else
  Will be found at life's close in the heart of a
    friend.

The Rainbow's End

What will we find at the close of Time,
  At the distant rainbow's end?
The pot of gold we had long dreamed of,
  Or love in the heart of a friend?

Will place and position be given us,
  Will our ears ring with plaudits wild?
Or will heart beat warm with a new found joy
  At the merry laugh of a child?

It is little thot we'll give these things:
  Gold and position and land,
We'd give it all and count it gain
  For the touch of Mother's hand.

Despise Not Little Things

Thou, God, who holdeth fast the universe in
    space;
Thou, God, who painteth bright the tiny wild
    flower's face·
This lesson I would learn of Thee—
Despise no thing—it matters not how small it be.

E'en tho my mind be filled with questions great,
Mayhap of Freedom's Cause, or Rule of State,
Let me not overlook the little things I find,
For acts as these bind closer all mankind.

If

If you had but one day to live,
I wonder how you'd live it?
Would you still scramble after power,
And wealth pursue in your last hour?
I wonder how you'd live it?

If you had but one loaf to share,
I wonder would you share it,
With one who hungered all alone,
Or would you offer such a stone?
I wonder would you share it?

If you had but one wish to make,
I wonder would you make it
A selfish one, meant all for you,
Or would you wish for my good, too?
I wonder what you'd make it?

Life's Problem

Today we are happy, tomorrow we're sad;
Today business good, while tomorrow it's bad;
Today life is rapture, tomorrow it's pain;
Today is all sunshine, tomorrow all rain;
Today we may smile, while tomorrow we frown;
Today we look upward, tomorrow look down;
Today do our best, on tomorrow our worst;
Today quaff of joy's cup, tomorrow athirst;
Today in a crowd and tomorrow alone;
Today we court pleasure, tomorrow atone;
Today we give comfort, tomorrow give pain,
So happy let's be, whether sunshine or rain.
Today we show courage, tomorrow we're weak;
Today we shun sin which tomorrow we seek;
Today life's a problem which tomorrow makes
    plain,
Then happy let's be, whether sunshine or rain.

Ye Who Pray

What are you asking for
  In your daily prayers,
Strength to perform your tasks
  Or surcease from your cares?

Gold, to gratify your wish,
  Or succor give to one
Who's missed the better things in life,
  Whose race is well nigh run?

Ask ye in selfish mood
  Just self to gratify,
Or ask ye for the good of all
  Who dwell beneath the sky?

Hear Ye in Mercy

The greatest sins within this land
   Are selfishness and greed;
We've overlooked these two great crimes;
   We give them little heed
While rushing madly day by day,
   Pursuing wealth and place;
We've nigh lost sight of Brotherhood
   In our relentless chase.

The less fortunate we crush
   Beneath our ruthless heel;
We've thot so long of just ourselves
   We've lost the power to feel
A pang of pity for the one
   Who lost in life's great game;
Who courted just a homely life;
   Not wealth, nor power, nor fame.

But now with old age creeping near,
   With no gold in his purse,
He asks for food and shelter warm,
   We answer with a curse;
Tho oft we've read his well writ lines
   And gazed on paintings rare,
We turn deaf ears and hurry on
   Nor heed this suppliant's prayer.

I wonder when the deeds of men
   Are judged by Him on High,
Who sees our every little act
   From throne there in the sky,
I wonder will our sordid gold
   Outweigh his work of art,
Who writ his lines and painted scenes
   With red blood from his heart.

What of the Harvest

I wonder who the winner is,
  When all is done and said,
The one who's toiling here today,
  Or he who's with the dead?
Is death reward for good deeds done,
  Or punishment for sin?
Is death the ending of our lives,
  Or does it just begin?

We're told that death down here on earth
  Is punishment bestowed
On those who choose the broad highway,
  Instead the narrow road.

But mayhap we in our poor way,
　As judge 'twixt wrong and right,
Have overlooked what death might hold
　In our poor blinded sight.

The seed we plant within the soil
　Decays ere it can bring
Of fruitage bearing life and strength,
　A lovely wondrous thing.
Thus death may be a stepping stone
　From all our cares and strife,
Into a broader, grander world,
　Into eternal life.

Give

If death should come today and claim
This house of clay in which I live,
I'd feel my life had been complete
Life's greatest lesson now I've learned
It is to give—to give.

Practice or Precept

How many of us practice absolute truth,
In our everyday lives today?
We say, " Yes, that's right,"
But when put to the test
Do the thing in our own selfish way.

We read a keen adage and say ''That sounds
    good,
That there's truth in each word 'twould convey,''
But the practice of it—
Aye, there is the rub,
So it's done in our own selfish way.

I wonder how many on reading this verse,
Will decide he'll begin it today,
And will practice the truth
He knows that is right,
Doing so in an unselfish way?

Love's Harvest

This little thot I give to you—
If to yourself you would be true,
If love you wish, of love bestow,
And love you'll find where'er you go.

For we shall reap of what we sow—
Of joy and gladness, pain or woe—
Let's sow of love: our harvest's sure,
If thoughts be right, and motives pure!

Just Folks

After all is said and done,
　We all are just plain folks.
Tho some boast riches—others power,
　Each may be lost within the hour:
Life's more or less a hoax.

A moment may efface the years
　Of toil and struggle drear,
We chance it all on pitch and toss,
　Of winning all or suffer loss
Without a thot of fear.

The're some who gain an honored name
　By years of watchful care;
When by chance word of friend or foe,
　A seed of doubt will quickly grow,
Bring ruin and despair.

Then let no one attempt to judge,
　Life's more or less a hoax;
Each has his faults, his virtues, too,
　About the same as I and you,
Just common, average folks.

Always Joy

*Look up, not down!   Just smile, not
    frown!
Our life is what we make it!
Forget the past—clouds cannot last—
    There's joy, if we but take it!*

You

If I can find you at the end of the lane,
What care I tho the journey be long,
Tho the clouds hover near, there is nothing to fear,
My heart will be filled with a song.

If I can find you at the end of the day,
What care I tho the labor be hard,
My work will be play; my night turned to day;
My progress will nothing retard.

If I can find you at the end of my life,
What care I when the Reaper appears,
For mine you will be thru eternity,
Where time is not counted by years.

Because of You

Because of You—the sun shines bright today
  And tho You're many, many miles away,
Your cheery messages so help,—
  Indeed they do;
And all my little world is glad—
  Because of You.

Somebody

Somebody once came into my life,
When I was discouraged and blue,
    Whose word of good cheer
    Dispelled every fear,
While the lilt of a song stanched the hot,
    bitter tear,
And that somebody, dear, was you.

Somebody once bid me but try once more
When the whole world it seemed was untrue.
    Tho I'd given my best,
    With vigor and zest,
Heartsick, and faith gone, I sought comfort
    and rest,
And that somebody, dear, was you.

Somebody once, when business was bad,
Smiled when all else seemed askew,
    And said, "Just forget,
    Don't worry nor fret,
Life's battle you'll win if it's but fairly met,"
And that somebody dear, was you.

A Love Song

My heart is singing a bit of a song,
Of twilight, of roseleaves, of dew,
Of soft winds, of starshine, the plaint of
songbird
Of a wonderful night—and You.

A Friend

The most wonderful thing in this world is
to have
A friend, who you know understands,
Who shows it in eyes and who lists it in voice,
Who throbs it in grasp of his hand.

Who sees all the good, who is blind to the bad,
Who shares in your sorrow or joy,
It matters not what, he judges you not,
Keeps the gold and forgets the alloy.

Who shares of his portion and asks not return,
Be it wealth, be it love, be it power,
Such a friend has a worth beyond wealth of
this earth—
A solace in life's darkest hour.

Who don't have to tell you in words he's your
friend,
It shows in each act he bestows,
Let come then what will, blow the wind good
or ill,
He never misjudges—he knows.

Memories

I caught the lilt of a song today,
That brought memories, Dear Heart, of you,
I again felt the touch of your pulsing hand,
With its firm clasp, warm and true.
All time and distance, were lost, Dear Heart,
I was wrapped in mem'rys thrall.
Was it you, Dear Heart, reaching out to me?
Was it your voice I heard call?

Longing

Here in this distant land I need you, dear,
  I need your words of courage bold,
    To cheer me as in days of old—
Your words that scatter every doubt and fear.

Here in this distant land I want you, dear.
  I hunger for the love of you,
    A love that's steadfast, warm and true—
Your love that dries each bitter, scalding tear.

Here in this distant land I call you, dear,
  Each morning at the rise of sun,
    And on and on till day is done
My lips keep calling, wishing you were here.

Here in this distant land I wait you, dear,
  I listen for your footsteps fall
    Along the summer garden's wall
I listen for the step that draws you near.

Friend-O-Mine

Friend-O-Mine, long miles between us lie,
As day by day I dream of days gone by,
And as I live in thot the hours spent with you,
I wonder—do you sometimes miss me, too?

Man O' Mine

There's not a word in the Universe
That means so much to me,
As the one word MAN, that's the biggest,
Is now and always will be.
A manly man, and an honest man,
A man with a cheery smile;
And such a man are you, my dear,
A man that's worth the while.

For Man O'Mine you cheer me so,
When everything goes dead wrong,
With your hand clasp true, smile in eyes o'blue,
With your whistle or cheery song;
You laugh at my fear. Say "Cheer up,
     my dear,"
Let us hold to the thot "I Can,"
Oh! what would I do, my dear, without you?
Man O'Mine, my Wonderful Man.

Heart O' Mine

Your presence, dear, came to me last night,
   As I lay half asleep,
Over a thousand miles of space,
   Sweet vigil with me to keep.
I wonder did you but feel response
   In answer to your heart's call?
Oh, heart o' Mine! I do love you,
   Your body, your soul, your all.

A Night In June

When I look in the heart of a rose, my dear,
   It's your sweet face I see,
With your lovelit eyes filled with glad surprise,
   Looking deep in the Soul of me.
And I long for the touch of your hand, my dear,
   For a walk 'neath the silvery moon,
And I whisper your name again, and again,
   As I dream of a night in June.

Communion

Every beat of your heart finds answer in mine,
As echo resounds from yon hill.
Vast distance means nothing,
Your soul reaches mine
Just now, and pray God ever will.

Pleading

These hungry, hungry hands o' mine
They're reaching out for you;
For touch of you, for feel of you,
Thrills my whole being thru and thru;
There's magic in your touch.

These hungry, hungry lips o' mine
Are calling out for you,
For word of yours, for praise of yours
A new lease on my life assures;
There's life in every word.

This hungry, hungry heart o' mine
Is pleading, dear, for you;
For heart of you, for soul of you,
For every word and thot of you;
For you, sweetheart, just you.

Old Friend

It's a long, long day since I saw your face
Saw you walking straight toward me
With your old accustomed grace.
But I've thought of you and longed for you
And wished it might come true,
Again to walk life's narrow path
With you, old friend, with you.

Days Are Lonely

Days are lonely, nights are drear
When you're absent Heart o'mine,
Sit and listen for your voice
Heart o'Mine, Heart o'mine.
Wander aimless 'bout the place
Honin' for you Heart o'Mine,
Everything seems new and strange,
Heart o'mine, Heart o' mine.

You'll be coming back some day
Back to me dear Heart o'mine,
And my face will shine with joy,
Heart o'mine, Heart o'mine.
Nevermore you'll leave me dear
Leave these arms dear Heart o'mine,
List! My lips are calling now
Heart o'mine, Heart o'mine.

A Hand Clasp

Here's my hand across the distance,
Wishes best I send;
Tho skies be bright or skies be gray,
Just count me as your friend.

Lonesome

Did you ever have a lonely feelin'
  stealin' 'round your heart,
An' spite of all sometimes, I jing!
  the tears would up and start?
You scarcely understand the cause
  that started them to flow—
You're lonesome! I've been there
  myself—I'm tellin' what I know.

It little odds where one may be;
  sometimes when I'm at home,
I've felt the demon of unrest,
  and then my heart would hone
For somethin' I could scarcely name
  and out o' doors I'd go
A-searchin' here and searchin' there—
  'twas lonesomeness, I know.

Sometimes I wonder what we'll find
  when we've left this earth.
Will we commence another life,
  a sort o' second birth?
If so, I hope there's one thing
  that will be forgotten there;
If lonesomeness is lost, I jing!
  I will not have a care.

Love's Faith

My faith in you, dear heart, is fixed,
As yon bright moon
That sweeps tonight across the starlit skies.
Tho all the world should come and say
That you were false to me,
I'd look into your eyes
And know, that time nor distance ne'er could
*   change*
Your steadfast love, that's mine, all mine tonight,
And mine will be
Thruout the Aeons of Eternity.

Three Little Words

All the day long, dear,
　All the night thru,
There's a song in my heart,
　And the song is of you.
List to its melody,
　Words are so few—
Just three little words, dear,
　They are—I love You.

When you're away, dear,
　Days are so long,
Awaiting your coming,
　I list for your song.
Come, dear, and meet me,
　I will be true,
These words will greet you,
　Just these—I love You.

Since You Came

There's a new strain of sweetness in the song
    bird's trill,
  There's an added glory in the skies;
For the sweetness is stolen from your love
    song, dear,
  And the glory from your love lit eyes.

There's a new joy in service since I found you,
    dear,
  There's a wish I might ease another's load;
For your words of cheer scatter every doubt
    and fear,
  As we journey down the long, long road.

Because of Your Love in My Heart

The sun in the Heavens shines brighter today,
  Because of your love in my heart;
The clouds' burnished gold and the skies'
    azure blue,
And it all came about for my great love for you,
  Because of your love in my heart.

The birds in the forest more sweetly now sing,
  Because of your love in my heart;
With melody rare each note breathes a prayer,
It banishes trouble and sorrow and care,
  Because of your love in my heart.

The flowers in the garden sweeter perfume exude,
  Because of your love in my heart;
With colors more bright than the glad stars by
    night,
To my tear bedimmed eyes, oh a glorious sight,
  Because of your love in my heart.

A Bit of A Smile

Just a bit of a smile you gave me, my friend,
  When my heart was heavy and sad,
Just a bit of a smile and a hand clasp so true,
Changed the dull leaden skies to a wonderful
    blue,
Filled my heart with a song—that was glad.

Some Day

Some of these days, dear, all things will be right,
As day follows ever the long dreary night,
So heaven we'll find here with us some day;
November's chill winds will be tempered by May.

Some of these days, dear, all joy will be ours,
Earth will be perfumed with sweet fragrant
   flowers,
Beauty we'll find then in things commonplace,
Made so by the glorious smile from your face.

Some of these days, dear, our dreams will
   come true,
Heaven 'twill mean, dear, to me and to you,
No more of parting and no more of pain;
Joy will be ours, dear, for Love then will reign.

Matters Not The Weather

What care we tho' north winds blow,
What care we tho' clouds hang low,
    If we be together
Sunshine's found where you are, dear,
Happiness is always near
    Matters not the weather.

Trinity

The sun would shine thru clouds of gray,
  If you were here, if you were here!
The night would all be turned to day,
  If you were here, if you were here.
No bitterness would mar our peace,
  Our hearts would join in one glad feast,
Our hands would clasp in close embrace,
  And leave of sorrow not a trace;
Our lips would meet in spite of fate,
  While soul would speak unto its mate.
Love, You, and I—O sacred treat,
  'Twould form a trinity complete,
'Twould scatter every doubt and fear,
  If you were here, if you were here.

Lonesome Folks

How many, many lonesome folks,
I come across each day,
I gather this from look in eyes,
Or something that they say.
Each searching for a loyal friend,
Someone who'll understand
Who'll give an answering response
To touch of hungry hand.

I Love You

Just to hear you say, ``I love you,``
  Just to see you smile,
Just to feel your presence near me,
  Makes life worth the while.

Just to feel your wondrous hand clasp,
  Just to touch your lips,
Sets my red blood pulsing madly
  Heart to finger tips.

Why Should We Be Parted

Friend o'mine the days are passing swiftly by,
Why should we be parted, you and I?
Life is short for love my dear,
Let us grasp what's left of it,
Let us live the rest of it,
Live it now and here.

Whither Thou Goest

Whither thou goest I will go,
All of life's journey thru;
Shoulder to shoulder and palm prest to palm,
Whether the pathway be stormy or calm,
I shall be happy, with you.

When thou rejoicest, I will rejoice,
All of life's journey thru,
Sorrow I'll share when it touches thy heart,
Joy be my portion when joyful thou art,
I shall be happy, with you.

My Star

I saw my star in the sky tonight,
In its field of azure blue,
It twinkled and smiled adown on me
My star, that means always—you;
'Twas the star that beamed on us, dear heart,
When you pledged mine own you'd be,
Each night since then when the world's asleep
It has guided and guarded me.

Starlight

Twilight is stealing o'er all the blue sky,
Venus is lighting her stars,
Glorious Luna is trimming her sails,
Agleam now is Saturn and Mars.
Stardust is falling, its glamor I feel
Tingling my heart and my brain;
Time is forgotten, the years brushed aside,
Youth's in my blood once again.

There's something in starlight that enters my
    blood,
That quickens my pulse as would wine;
There's a witchery found neath the bright
    milky way,
There's a something akin the Divine.
'Tis a mingling of tears and of laughter and song,
Of pathos, of passion, of love,
That quickens my heartbeat, that brings back
    my youth
When the stars shed their light from above.

A Real Friend

It's a friend o' mine I'm thinking of,
A real friend, tried and true,
A friend I'm wishing for right now,
The friend? Why that is you.

His Love Can Be Seen In Everything

The Gates of the Holy City
I saw in the skies tonight,
When the sun dipped low in the westland,
With its purple and golden light.

God's voice I heard from the tree tops,
Reflected in songbirds' trill,
By soughing of breeze in the forest,
Rippling water by wayside mill.

His strength is portrayed by the ocean,
His grandeur in mountains tall,
While his tenderness shows in his watchful care
As he notes e'en the sparrows fall.

For God is found all about us
Instead of far distant skies,
And His love can be seen in everything,
If we only will open our eyes.

Red Roses

These roses, red with fragrance rare,
Last night were bathed in dew,
They gathered sweetness and perfume
For you, sweetheart—for you!

They yielded up their very lives,
And murmured not, I ween,
To deck the brow of one I love—
Of you, my sweetheart—queen.

Melody

Listen to my heart a singin'
Singin' cause of you,
Yesterday the skies were gray,
Now they're azure blue.
Come, I'll tell you now the reason,
Tell you why it's true;
'Cause I'm comin' dearie,
Comin' back to you.

I have been so lonely, dearie,
Since we've been apart,
Had a sorto choky feelin'
Stealin' round my heart.
Now its gone and left me,
Not a trace of blue,
And it's 'cause I'm comin' dearie,
Comin' back to you.

Sometime in the future, dearie,
We shall part no more,
But our lives will be united,
As in days of yore.
Every day I'm honin' for you,
Scarce know what to do,
Now I'm comin' dearie,
Comin' back to you.

The Daisy

This daisy's face I kissed, sweetheart,
  And thot of your face true;
I'm hungering now for your sweet lips,
  For eyes of wondrous blue.

Its heart of gold can ne'er compare
  With your heart, sweetheart, mine;
Its face turned ever toward the sun,
  I've likened unto thine.

Sweetheart of Mine

Sweetheart of mine, my heart still is calling;
  Can you not hear it sometimes in the night
After the day with its labor has ended,
  When the stars shine in the heavens so bright?

Sweetheart, I need you, I need your dear presence,
  I grow disheartened with toil and with care;
Come when I'm sleeping, or come when I'm
    waking;
  Kiss me on eyelids, on lips, and on hair!

My arms are aching just now to enfold you;
  My lips are hungry for your kisses sweet;
My eyes are eager just now to behold you;
  Come, and your coming will make life complete.

When You Come

Gray skies, tear wet eyes,
  Gee! but I'm lonesome tonight;
Hear my heart sighin', see my eyes cryin',
  Come, dear, and all will be right.

Sunlight, eyes bright,
  Gee! but I'm happy to-day;
Hear my lips hummin', my sweetheart's
    comin',
  Clouds are all driven away.

Gratitude

To you, who to my hungry heart
    A feast of love have brot,
I bow today in gratitude—
    With patience you have taught.
The greatest truths, and courage giv'n
    To one, who'd wearied grown,
Who'd missed the better things in life,
    Who'd travelled all alone.

A beauty new I gather now
    From things quite commonplace;
New chords of harmony I catch,
    New lines of beauty trace!
I've learned we find in life each day
    The thing we most desire,
And by a kindly word and deed
    Discouraged souls inspire.

I've found in you, dear heart of mine,
    A love that satisfies;
A rainbow bright, you've painted, dear,
    In sombre darkened skies.
And so I bow in gratitude,
    I bless the hour and day,
That brot you to my lonely life,
    And scattered fears away.

Yearning for You

The silvery moon is shining
  In the heavens up above,
While my heart for you is pining,
  Longing, sweetheart, for your love!
In my fancy I can see you
  With your love-lit eyes so true,
Brighter than the stars above me,
  Set in ground of azure blue!

Oh! the days we've spent together!
  I recall them every one;
Not a cloud with you beside me;
  Your smile coaxes out the sun,
But the days pass by so slowly,
  When we're parted, sweetheart mine,
And my heart cries out to see you,
  When I see the old moon shine!

A Withered Flower

On a pavement hot on a city's street,
   I found a flower today,
Dropped there methinks by some careless hand,
   Or thoughtlessly cast away.
It looked so pleadingly up to me,
   As I hurried down the street,
It seemed somehow like an old time friend,
   One we're always glad to meet.
And when I stooped and picked it up,
   It seemed to me it smiled
And twined itself 'bout my finger tips,
   As would hand of a lonely child.
I placed it gently in book of mine,
   Among names of my friends so true,
And it cheered my lonely heart all day,
   So I'm sending the thot to you.

Side By Side

I wonder what we shall find, Old Pal,
When we leave these trails down here?
Somehow I think we'll ride side by side,
Our hearts bubbling o'er with cheer.

Methinks I can hear your merry laugh,
As we race up the milky way,
A wondering where we shall strike our camp
At the close of a joyous day.

The trials and problems we found here on earth,
Will be plain as a beaten trail,
And we'll laugh and forget without single regret,
In the Land of the Holy Grail.

I Wonder the Reason Why

One day in center of grassland patch,
  I saw a lonely tree;
While not another did meet my gaze
  As far as my eye could see.
Its leaves had fallen, yet proud it stood,
  Each branch pointed toward the sky,
And somehow it seemed a part of me,
  I wonder the reason why?

I heard the plaint of a songbird's trill,
  A bird who had lost its mate,
While sorrow it seemed to echo low
  Without one hint of complaint.
Then with flutter of wing it mounted swift
  Toward the vast domain of the sky,
And the bird and the song seemed a part of me,
  I wonder the reason why?

I saw a man in a city's street,
  'Mid countless throngs of folk,
Yet he seemed alone as on prairies broad,
  For none to him smiled nor spoke.
Then his thots turned back to the grassland patch,
  And to bird in the clear blue sky,
And his heartstrings thrilled and his sad eyes
    filled,
  I wonder the reason why?

Pal o' Mine

Pal o' mine, Pal o' mine,
  Comrade, chum and friend,
Shoulders touch, this means much,
  Work and play we'll blend.

Pal o' mine, Pal o' mine,
  Hand clasp ever true,
Words of cheer ever dear
  I would speak to you.

Pal o' mine, Pal o' mine,
  Onward then we'll go,
Summer hours strewn with flowers,
  Happiness we'll sow.

Pal o' mine, Pal o' mine,
  We'll ne'er know defeat,
Courage show, upward go,
  Life will be complete.

The Inspiring West

There's something about this Westland,
  Found in mountains and prairies broad,
That lifts one's soul from the sordid earth
  Right up to the Gates of God.
It never is found in the cities,
  Filled with pretense, with sham and unrest,
But it's found underneath the blue arch of the sky
  In this wonderful, heart throbbing West.

The Lure of the Hills

There is an intangible something,
That in spring time my heart strangely thrills,
A something that calls me, that woos me,
I call it the Lure of the Hills.

For when duty demands every moment,
Or when sorrow my cup more than fills,
My thoughts steal away to a long summer day,
When I courted the Lure of the Hills.

Mountain Pine

Pray tell me mountain pine
  Who gave thee birthplace there,
Far up on rugged mountain side
  With head poised high in air?

Tell me of winters braved,
  Of mountain torrents wild,
Of lightnings flash, of thunders roll,
  Of summer breezes mild?

Who nurtured when fierce ray
  Of sun beat down on thee?
Who watered thee when lips were parched?
  Pray tell me mountain tree!

Due homage I would pay
  To thee who's stood the test,
For next to God and next to man
  Brave tree, I love thee best.

In Memory of a Summer Day

*In memory of a summer day when our trails
 ran side by side,
Mayhap no more Old Pal o` Mine till we cross
 the Great Divide,
And if this be our lot, Old Pal,
May our meeting be as sweet
As `twas today on mountain crest,
`And life will be complete.*

The Mountain Stream

Where art thou going Mountain Stream
Rushing so madly along,
With your swish and your roar,
With your mighty downpour,
With your never ending song?

Tell me thy source, dear Mountain Stream,
Tell me who gave thee birth?
Was it cloud or spring
Started thy mad fling?
Art thou child of the sky or earth?

I'm hurrying onward to parched plain
While my song is a song of love;
My source is a never ending one,
'Tis from God who ruleth the earth and sun,
The Omnipotent God above.

Wonderful Days

These are wonderful days,
In a wonderful clime,
'Neath a wonderful sky of blue,
But more wonderful still,
Would be lakeside and hill,
Were you here to enjoy it, too.

The Mountain Peak

Huge Mountain Peak towers high above my head,
Grim monument to pioneer long dead,
While gold and blue crown peak with colors rare,
And pungent scent of pine tree fills the air.
No sound is heard save rustling of the leaves
Of quaking aspen.   Let him who still believes
There is no God, come stand beside me now,
Methinks his head in reverence would bow
And praise to God omnipotent,
He'd voice with trembling lip,
While gold and violet would crown
Yon mountain's highest tip.

A Prairie Portrait

Early morn on the prairies! what artist could
  paint it?
  The gold and the purple, the crimson, the blue,
The mists slowly rising, the darkness receding,
  Chased back by bright colors of every known
  hue!

The dew in the meadows is glistening like
  diamonds,
  The air is as sweet as a rose newly born,
While the wheat is fast turning to yellow, so
  golden,
  Interspersed with broad fields of emerald
  corn!

The sunflower bright to the east now is facing,
  As tho it would worship its namesake, I ween,
While the brook, singing low on its way to the
  ocean,
  Takes on a bright color of silvery sheen!

In the West

I've been thinking today of the gladness
Found with you—Friend so true
     In the West.
Of the joy that was there,
Of freedom from care
In the life-giving, love living West.

I've been wishing today for the sunshine
Radiant fair—every where
     In the West.
Of the breeze sweet and cool,
Of the stream and the pool,
In the heart thrilling, soul filling West.

I've been longing today for the mountains
Towering high—toward the sky
     In the West.
Strength they give to the weak,
Words of courage they speak,
In the God giving, real living West.

A Toast to the Pioneers

Hats off to the Early Pioneers,
  Who conquered our prairies broad!
It took a lot of stick-to-it-ive-ness
  And a heap o' faith in God
When drouth and hoppers and wind and
    sand
  Came to try out their mettle and worth,
These Pioneers stuck in spite of it all—
  Hats off, to these Kings of Earth!

A Prairie Vision

Miles on miles of level prairies,
  Stretch before my vision broad,
Breathes of freedom, boundless freedom,
  Shows the handiwork of God!

Not a tree, and not a mountain,
  Nothing to obstruct one's view;
Earth's all carpeted with emerald,
  Vaulted o'er with sky of blue!

Flowers grow in thick profusion,
  Gold and purple, pink and white,
And the perfume from their blossoms,
  Fill my soul with keen delight!

Autumn Days

Oh, the glories of the forest on these bright
    autumnal days,
When colors of the leaves surpass the rainbow's
    beauteous rays;
When tang of burning stalk and leaf is borne
    upon the air,
No scene mid cycle of the year can to these days
    compare.

My Heart's Calling for You

Out in the land where the sunflower grows,
Where the sun always shines,
Where the wind always blows,
Where the air's always sweet;
Where the sky's always blue,
Oh! fair, sunny Kansas,
My heart's calling for you!

Here in the city 'midst dust, and 'midst
smoke,
Where the day after pay
We're always dead broke,
Where all's chasing the dollar,
Where real friends are few,
I'm homesick for Kansas,
My heart's calling for you!

The World Is Fair

A summer shower we had today.
   The flowers are smiling everywhere!
The birds still sing, while on the wing,
    "The world is fair! The world is fair!"

The sky is flecked with clouds of gold,
   (Such beauty is, indeed, most rare!)
While breezes blow, and whisper low,
    "The world is fair! The world is fair!"

All Nature seems to be at peace,
   The bees are humming here and there;
At work all day they seem to say
    "The world is fair! The world is fair!"

When trouble seems to fill all space,
   When life is filled with woe and care,
May we, too, sing like birds on wing,
    "The world is fair! The world is fair!"

Let not the mistakes of yesterday,
Nor the fear of tomorrow,
Spoil thy today.

The day is finished,
All tasks undone remain undone,
For each succeeding day brings problems new
That brain and brawn doth task
Till setting of the sun.

The one thing—the great thing—
The thing that makes man free—
Is love of God, and love of Man,
And love of Liberty.

Cultivate smiling; returns are sure and their worth greater than much gold.

A grin's worth while,
But a smile is better,
While a cheery laugh
Is a business getter.

Try forgetting the word forgot—put remember in its place.

Try letting your heart, instead of your head, handle your charities—you'll sleep sounder.

Try leaving unsaid an unkind thot and you'll not need to consult the beauty doctor.

Try gaining love by giving love and you'll find an hundredfold increase.

Know this—
That into thy heart God has placed power
To meet life's problems, hour by hour.

Pray not for wealth, nor Power, nor Ease,
But rather ask that strength and wisdom be given
      you
Whereby you may acquire these.

The truly beautiful is seen only through
The eyes of love, for love glorifies all.

I would judge man's love for God by the treatment he affords his fellow man.

He who would succeed must give the best that in him lies, if recompense of vital worth be his as just reward.

A man's bigness may well be measured by the little things he is willing to do.

When about to let go—hold on!

Why waste thy life in search of sordid gold
When all along thy path lie riches of far
      greater value,
A legal tender here on earth,
An open sesame thru all worlds to come?

CPSIA information can be obtained
at www.ICGtesting.com
Printed in the USA
LVHW082022110720
660413LV00008B/273

9 781010 087038